Madam President

Five Women Who Paved the Way

Published by Eifrig Publishing,
PO Box 66, Lemont, PA 16851, USA
Knobelsdorffstr. 44, 14059 Berlin, Germany.

For information regarding permission, write to:
Rights and Permissions Department,
Eifrig Publishing,
PO Box 66, Lemont, PA 16851, USA.
permissions@eifrigpublishing.com, +1-888-340-6543

Library of Congress Cataloging-in-Publication Data
 Gutgold, Nichola D. and Abigail S. Kennedy

Madam President: Five Women Who Paved the Way /
by Nichola D. Gutgold and Abigail Kennedy, illustrated by Jane Ramsey

p. cm.

Paperback: ISBN 978-1-63233-035-2
Hard cover: ISBN 978-1-63233-036-9

[1. Biography/Women - Juvenile non-Fiction. 2. US Presidents - Juvenile non-Fiction.]

I. Ramsey, Jane , ill. II. Title

19 18 17 16 2015
5 4 3 2 1

Printed on recycled acid-free paper. ∞

We have had over forty presidents
in the United States since the country began,
and all of them have been men. But did you
know that many women have also run for president?
They have been trying for decades and will keep trying
until they succeed. Sometime soon a woman will be
elected president of the United States.

It could be you!

Margaret Chase Smith
ran for President of the United States in 1964

While Margaret Chase was still in elementary school, to pay for the things she wanted, she started working at a five-and-dime store and helping out at her father's barbershop. Margaret liked staying busy and feeling independent. In everything she did, she was a leader. She also loved to play basketball, and when she graduated from high school she became a coach for her high school's team. Later, Margaret worked as a telephone operator and a newspaper writer, and she got involved in professional women's clubs.

She married Clyde Smith, who became a **congressman**, and she became politically active too. When Clyde became ill, he suggested that she run for his seat, which she did, and she won uncontested in 1940.

In 1948, **Congresswoman** Margaret Chase Smith then ran for **senator** and won in a landslide. The only woman among 99 men in the entire United States Senate, Margaret worked hard to be heard. There weren't even women's rest rooms near the floors of the Senate and House of Representatives in the Capital Building, where the members of Congress would meet and vote on laws. She had to walk ten minutes to the tourist section to use the facilities. But Margaret did not let **inequalities** like that stop her from succeeding.

When she cared about something, she bravely spoke out when no other **senator** would, and people started to notice her. In one of her most famous speeches, she said, "I speak simply and briefly in the hope that my words will be taken to heart." Her words did have a big impact on the country, and she received many letters asking her to run for president.

Just like when she was young and wanted to earn her own money, she decided she would use her own funds instead of others' for her presidential campaign. She told people that by running for president, even though she might not win, she would be helping a woman get elected in the future. If nothing else, she said she wanted to "make the way easier" for a woman to someday become president.

Go for your dreams, because even if you don't succeed, you may inspire others to try things that seem out of reach.

What do you dream of doing?

Shirley Anita St. Hill Chisholm

ran for President of the United States in 1972

When Shirley St. Hill was a young girl, she and her two sisters went to the island of Barbados to live with their grandmother while her parents worked in New York. Her parents wanted to earn enough money to buy their own home and to send their daughters to college. Shirley's grandmother was strict, but very loving, insisting that Shirley and her sisters take education seriously.

Accepting nothing less than full effort, Shirley's grandmother helped teach a strong **work ethic**.

After a few years of **diligent** schoolwork, Shirley and her sisters returned to the United States, where they were at the top of their classes. When Shirley graduated from college, she looked very young, and

people hesitated to hire her. Shirley had to speak up for herself and prove she could work hard.

Shirley found work as a teacher and a director at a childcare center. From her school she could see city hall, and it inspired her to get involved in her community. Soon Shirley began attending city hall meetings. From there, she ran for Congress and won.

People liked to listen to her unafraid and passionate speeches. Shirley even said, "I have a way of speaking that does something to people." She was right.

When Shirley Chisholm ran for president, lots of people came to hear her speak. She said, "Our time has come in America. We can't accept things the way they are."

She talked to kids everywhere about how important it is to work hard in school and get a good education. Just seeing a black woman run for president inspired many African Americans to achieve their dreams, even when others said they couldn't.

What would you like to try that you might think is too difficult?

Patricia Scott Schroeder

ran for President of the United States in 1988

Patricia Scott, or "Pat" to her friends and family, was born in Oregon, but she moved around the country due to her father's job in the airline industry. As a young girl, Pat's parents taught her **persistence**. Pat was born with an eye **defect**, and when doctors told her father she might be blind by the age of five, her dad refused to accept that. He traveled all around the country seeking medical care for her.

Her parents also taught her the importance of saving money. In elementary school, each month her parents gave her a small allowance for her lunch and things she wanted.

15

Pat learned that if she spent it all too quickly, she would not have any money leftover at the end of the month. It was a valuable lesson that served her well throughout her life.

When Pat Scott was a young girl, she wanted to fly. She followed her dream and earned her pilot's license at fifteen. Piloting planes helped to pay her way through college at the University of Minnesota. She even saved up enough money to pay for Harvard Law School, where she met her future husband, Jim Schroeder.
All of their friends and family thought that Jim would become a politician, but he wanted Pat to run for Congress. She did, and she became the first **congresswoman** to be in office with young children.

Pat Schroeder served twenty-four years in Congress, working for things that she cared about, such as childcare and other family issues, as well as improving benefits, **healthcare**, and living conditions for people in the military. During her presidential campaign, she talked about these issues with Americans around the country. Some policies in Washington D.C. frustrated her, and Pat wanted leaders to be more open with the public.

When she ran for president, she offered people honesty and common sense. After her presidential campaign, she toured the country with the Great American Family Tour, speaking about ideas on how to better raise a family.

Public speaking is a way to share ideas about important issues with others. What would you like to speak out about?

Elizabeth Hanford Dole

ran for President of the United States in 2000

When Elizabeth Hanford was growing up in North Carolina, her mother always encouraged her to be involved in community service and to always try her best. "Liddy," as she was called, loved being a

leader and being involved. She entered essay contests, read many books, and served as president of her third grade bird club. Her classmates admired her and voted her "Most likely to succeed." She served as president of her freshman class in high school

and was elected student body president at Duke University, as well, where she had quickly become a campus leader. After graduating, Elizabeth wanted to continue with her education.

19

While teaching at a high school, Elizabeth earned her master's degree in education from Harvard University. Still, she didn't think her education was complete. She met with Margaret Chase Smith. (Remember her?) She was the only woman in the Senate at the time, so Elizabeth asked her for career advice. She took Senator Smith's suggestions and earned another degree at Harvard Law School.

President Reagan **appointed** her **Secretary of Transportation**, the first woman to hold that position. Elizabeth also worked as the Secretary of Labor and president of the American Red Cross. Elizabeth is married to Senator Bob Dole, who was a presidential candidate himself in 1996. When Elizabeth Dole ran for president, she said, "My presidency would make the kind of history that would **reverberate** around the world." Even though she did not win, Elizabeth addressed important issues, such as improving **healthcare** and education.

Later, Elizabeth ran for a seat in the Senate in her home state of North Carolina, and won. As senator, Elizabeth was able to continue working to improve the lives of others.

Are there any issues in the world that are important to you? Do you want to make a difference in other people's lives? What changes would you like to help create?

Hillary Rodham Clinton
ran for President of the United States in 2008

Young Hillary Rodham dreamed of becoming an astronaut. She wrote to NASA, but was informed that this was not an option for women. Even that disappointment did not stop her goals for academic excellence.

Later, Hillary decided she could make an impact in a different way: she could help people through government. Hillary was **diligent** in her studies at Wellesley College. At graduation, she was the first student to give the **commencement speech**, in which she encouraged her classmates to practice what she called "the art of making the impossible possible."

Starting during her college days at Wellesley, she began researching poverty, community development, and especially the unfair treatment of women and girls around the world.

After graduating from Yale Law School, where she met her husband, Bill Clinton, Hillary worked as a successful lawyer at a firm in Arkansas. When Bill became the state's Governor, Hillary started working to improve education, **healthcare**, and legal services for kids.

When Bill became the forty-second president of the United States, as First Lady, Hillary, strong and independent, traveled to more than 80 countries doing **philanthropic** work. Later, she was elected to the Senate, where she served from 2001 to 2009.

In 2008, Hillary ran for president, receiving over 18 million votes, almost winning the Democratic bid. She made it further along the trail to the U.S. presidency than any other woman in history. Her concerns were important issues, such as **healthcare**, taxes, and the military.

Hillary Clinton received a lot of attention in the media. Sometimes reporters commented on her hairstyle or her choice of clothes instead of what was most important: her vision for America.

Hillary Clinton did not let the press get in her way. She kept campaigning to communicate what she truly believed.

When President Obama **appointed** her Secretary of State, she traveled to 112 countries to be of service to people all around the world.

No matter what obstacles lie ahead, it is important never to give up. What have you tried to do unsuccessfully that you would like to try again?

These are five women who attempted to become president of the United States, but they are not the only ones. The real question is, who will make it? Will it be someone you know? Could it be you?

Think about it!

1. What did each of these women do in school that helped prepare them to run for president?

2. Do you speak up in class?

3. When these women were told "no," what did they do?

4. What steps can you take to start reaching for your dreams?

5. Is there a woman in your life who inspires you?

While in the United States there has not yet been a Madam President, there have been many women leaders around the world. Here are just a few of them:

Presidents:

Corazon Aquino, Philippines
Michelle Bachelet, Chile
Agatha Barbara, Malta
Violeta Chamorro, Nicaragua
Cristina Fernández de Kirchner, Argentina
Vigdís Finnbogadóttir, Iceland
Park Geun-hye, South Korea
Dalia Grybauskaite, Republic of Lithuania
Ellen Johnson Sirleaf, Liberia
Chandrika Kumaratunga, Sri Lanka
Isabel Martínez de Perón, Argentina
Pratibha Patil, India
Mary Robinson, Ireland
Dilma Rousseff, Brazil
Megawati Sukarnoputri, Indonesia

Prime Ministers:

A prime minister is the most senior minister of cabinet in the executive branch of government in a parliamentary system.

Alenka Bratusek, Slovenia
Gro Harlem Brundtland, Norway
Kim Campbell, Canada
Indira Gandhi, India
Sheikh Hasina, Bangladesh
Golda Meir, Israel
Angela Merkel, Germany (Chancellor)
Kamla Persad-Bissessar, Trinidad and Tobago
Jenny Shipley, New Zealand
Portia Simpson Miller, Jamaica
Margaret Thatcher, United Kingdom
Helle Thorning-Schmidt, Denmark
Yulia Tymoshenko, Ukraine

Women who have run for President of the United States

1872	Victoria Woodhull
1884	Belva Lockwood
1964	Margaret Chase Smith
1972	Patsy Mink
1972	Shirley Chisholm
1976 and 1980	Ellen McCormack
1984	Sonia Johnson
1988	Patricia "Pat" Schroeder
1988 and 1992	Lenora Fulani
2000	Elizabeth Dole
2004	Carol Mosley Braun
2008	Hillary Rodham Clinton

Glossary

Appoint: to assign someone to a position. When Elizabeth Dole was appointed to Secretary of Transportation, she was assigned to that job.

Commencement speech: the opening or beginning speech given by an important speaker at a graduation

Congressman/Congresswoman: a member of the House of Representatives, one of the two groups of the United States Congress. A congressman or congresswoman can also be called a Representative. The other group is the Senate. Members of both groups make and pass laws.

Defect: something that doesn't look or work the way it should. When Pat Schroder had an eye defect, she had a problem with her eye that made her eye not work the way it should.

Diligent: showing a strong and steady effort and care for something. Someone who is diligent works hard.

Healthcare: the field that involves taking care of people's health. Doctors, nurses, and pharmacists are examples of people who work in healthcare in hospitals and pharmacies to improve people's health. Many politicians, such as the women in this book, have worked on laws to help improve healthcare in America.

Inequalities: things that are unfair or unequal. Margaret Chase Smith faced many inequalities, things that weren't fair, when she was a congresswoman.

Persistence: the act of working hard or lasting for a very long time. When Pat Schroder's parents taught her persistence, they taught her the value of working very hard for the things she wants and to not give up easily.

Philanthropic: being concerned about other's welfare and sharing one's time and money to improve the quality of life of others

Reverberate: to continue, last, or echo. When Elizabeth Dole said her presidency would make history that would reverberate around the world, she meant that her presidency would have an effect that would ring around the world.

Secretary of Transportation: One of the president's important advisors on issues related to transportation. The president has other Secretaries who advise him on other issues like Education, Defense, Agriculture, and more.

Senator: a member of the Senate, one of the two groups of the United States Congress. The other group of Congress is the House of Representatives. Members of both groups make and pass laws.

Work Ethic: a belief that hard work is important and necessary for a person.

ABOUT THE AUTHORS:

Nichola D. Gutgold is professor of communication arts and sciences at the Pennsylvania State University and associate dean of academic affairs at Schreyer Honors College. She has written passionately about women in non-traditional roles in her books: *Paving the Way for Madam President; Seen and Heard: The Women of Television News and Almost Madam President; The Rhetoric of Supreme Court Women; Almost Madam President* and *Gender and the American Presidency: Nine Presidential Women and the Barriers They Faced.* She has been quoted in the national and international press and has appeared on C-Span's Book TV. She has interviewed many of the women profiled in her books and her polling work has revealed a need to educate young people on the role of women in the United States, specifically the women who have tried to become President of the United States. She earned a PhD in speech communication from Penn State.

Abigail S. Kennedy is a Schreyer Honors College Scholar at the Pennsylvania State University. She plans to double major in English Literature and Secondary Education with minors in History and Latin American Studies. At Penn State, Abigail is a Lion Scout Tour Guide, a member of the Coda Conduct a cappella choir, and a member of the Schreyer Honors College Student Council. She is currently working on a novel on US intervention in Guatemala during the latter half of the twentieth century. In her spare time, Abigail enjoys reading anything and everything, playing piano, and spending time with her dog, Toby.

ABOUT THE ILLUSTRATOR:

Jane Ramsey recalls a childhood filled with endless hours of sketching and several years of travel and living in Micronesia and American Samoa where her parents were teachers. Study at Cornish College of the Arts in Seattle prepared her to become a graphic designer and illustrator, first working for a small agency, later opening her own studio. Today finds her freelancing and pursuing her passion for plein air watercolor. Her favorite subjects are barns and farmland. Whether creating art for the printed page or the frame, Jane's goal is to capture the spirit of each place and to tell a story.

Whoever that first woman president will be owes gratitude to her sisters who went before her.

–Nichola Gutgold

ACKNOWLEDGMENTS

Nichola D. Gutgold

Gratitude to my husband, Geoff, for his encouragement, and our wonderful (grown-up) children, Ian and Emily: I remember vividly the time we spent reading books together. They were the best of times.

Abigail S. Kennedy

Much love and thanks to Mama, Dad, Maggs, and Dys. The support, whether in hugs, advice, or jokes has been a lifeline.

Jane Ramsey

To my parents who instilled in me a love of books and encouraged my art, but most of all who made me believe that I could accomplish anything I set my mind and heart on. To Guy, my husband, best friend, supporter, and to Caroline, our daughter who is already pursuing her passion – horses! And finally, to Nikki, for generously inviting me to join her in creating this special book. Thank you.

CPSIA information can be obtained at www.ICGtesting.com
Printed in the USA
LVOW02s1058130215

426934LV00025B/379/P